NAUTICAL MUSEUM

DIRECTORY

4th Edition

W9-CFH-047

An Illustrated Directory Listing Nautical Museums
and Preserved Vessels in the United States and Canada.

DISCOUNT COUPONS

Guest coupons now enable you and your family to
obtain reduced admission fees at several of the sites
listed in the Directory.

Published by

QUADRANT PRESS, INC.

ISBN-0-915276-07-0

FOR YOUR INFORMATION

Listings   All nautical sites in this 4th Edition will be open as stated herein to the best knowledge of the Editors. Additional operations, still in the construction stage, will be eligible for listing in the 5th Edition.

Index   An alphabetical index will be found on Page 83.

Accuracy   Every effort has been made to ensure the accuracy of the contents. The Editors, however, are totally dependent upon the information supplied by the listing source. No responsibility can be assumed for errors, omissions or schedule changes.

Additional Copies   Available from Quadrant Press at $2.25 each. Dealers welcome, wholesale order blank on request.

1971, 1972 & 3rd Eds.   Still available at $1.75 per copy.

5th Edition Directory   To be published in 1978, cost $2.50 per copy. New listings are welcome. For information contact Quadrant Press.

Advertising   Advertising space for the next Nautical Museum Directory and the other topical directories published by Quadrant Press may now be reserved. Rates furnished upon request.

Brochures   Most listings in this Directory offer free brochures or other printed information. For prompt service, please enclose stamped, self-addressed envelope when writing for data.

Suggestions   The Editors welcome comments and suggestions regarding this Directory. Information on listings not included is most welcome.

Other Topical Directories   Quadrant Press publishes four other topical directories in the same format as the Nautical Museum Directory. The titles are Automobile Museum Directory, Restored Village Directory, Aircraft Museum Directory and American Revolution Bicentennial Directory, available at the same price as this book.

Address all correspondence to:

QUADRANT PRESS, INC.
Suite 707, 19 West 44th Street
New York, N. Y. 10036
Telephone (212) 490-1622

2

Location: On Battleship Parkway (U.S. 90) in Mobile.

Vessels: Two vessels are berthed in the Memorial Park at the head of Mobile Bay. The 43,500-ton USS Alabama (BB-60) was built at the Naval Shipyard in Norfolk, Virginia in 1942. In 1943, it joined the British Home Fleet in the North Atlantic for three months and then continued its service in the Pacific until the end of World War II, earning a total of nine battle stars. It was decommissioned in 1947 and became an Alabama State shrine in 1965. The Submarine USS Drum (SS-228) also saw service in the Pacific during World War II. She completed thirteen patrols, sank fifteen Japanese ships and was awarded twelve campaign stars. The 1525-ton submarine was constructed in Portsmouth, New Hampshire in 1941.

Schedule: Daily, year round, 8:00 A. M. to sunset.

Admission: Adults $2.00, Children 50c, under 6 free.
Group rate available.

√Refreshments	USS Alabama Battleship Commission
√Gift Shop	P.O. Box 65
√Free Parking	Mobile, Alabama 36601
√Picnic Area	Phone (205) 433-2703
	Capt. F. H. Brumby, U.S.N. (ret.), Director

Harry Merrick

Location: At Pier J near downtown Long Beach at the end of the Long Beach Freeway.

Vessels: The Queen Mary was built by John Brown & Co. of Clydebank, Scotland. The 81,237-ton ship was launched in September 1934 and began her maiden voyage during May 1936. From 1940-1946, the ship was on war duty and returned to its Atlantic run in July 1947. She made her last regular voyage in 1967 and arrived in Long Beach in December of that year. In addition to the hotel, many restaurants and shops aboard, there are three main attractions. These are the Queen Mary Museum, with exhibits on the ship and its equipment, an Upper Decks Tour and Cousteau's Living Sea. The latter features a three-level marine exhibition on underwater life and exploration.

Schedule: Tour: Daily, year round, 10:00 A. M. to 3:30 P. M.
Open until 4:30 P. M. on weekends and holidays.

Admission: Ticket to ship tour and exhibits:

Adults $4.00, Children (5-11) $1.75, under 5 free.

√Hotel	California Museum of the Sea Foundation
√Refreshments	P.O. Box 20890
√Restaurants	Long Beach, Calif. 90801
√Gift Shops	Phone (213) 435-4747
√Parking $1.00	Robert J. Reardon, Director

4

Allen Knight Maritime Museum

Location: At 550 Calle Principal in Monterey.

Exhibits: Opened in 1971, the Museum started with the large collection of nautical artifacts and relics accumulated by the late Allen Knight of Carmel. Since opening, much additional material has been added. There are about 50 ship models as well as exhibits of scrimshaw, navigation instruments, steering wheels and numerous other maritime items. In addition to prints and paintings of ships, one can see a large selection of nautical photographs. A comprehensive maritime library is open to researchers. The Allen Knight Museum is sponsored by the Monterey History and Art Association, Ltd., a non-profit organization.

Schedule: Daily, except Mondays, year round, June 15 to Sept. 15, Tuesday-Friday, 10:00 A. M. to Noon and 1:00 P. M. to 4:00 P. M. Weekends, 2:00 P. M. to 4:00 P. M. Rest of year, open only during afternoon hours. Closed National Holidays.

Admission: Free.
   Group tours arranged upon request.

Special Events: Monthly lectures on maritime subjects.

√Gift Shop
√City Parking

Allen Knight Maritime Museum
P.O. Box 805
Monterey, Calif. 93940
Phone (408) 375-2553
   R. Adm. Earl E. Stone, USN (Ret.), Director
√Memberships available on request.

Location: The vessels are situated on the waterfront at 1306 N. Harbor Drive in San Diego.

Vessels: Star of India — The oldest merchant vessel afloat. Launched in 1863 as the British ship Euterpe, she sailed for many years between England, India, Australia, and New Zealand. Sold to Hawaiian interests at the turn of the century; she came under United States registry with the annexation of Hawaii. Acquired by Alaska Packers Association in 1902 and sailed annually to Alaskan cannery ports until the mid-twenties.

Berkeley — Pride of the San Francisco ferry fleet until superseded by the Bay Bridge. Acquired by the Maritime Museum Association in 1973 and now being restored to house an increasing number of exhibits.

Medea — One of the few surviving steam yachts. Built in England, in 1904. Acquired, restored, and presented to the Association by Mr. Paul Whittier, in 1973.

Schedule: Daily, 9:00 A. M. to 8:00 P. M.

Admission: Adults $2.00, Servicemen (active) $1.50, Children under 12 50c, under 5 free.

Group rates available.

√Gift Shop
√City Parking

Maritime Museum Association of San Diego
(Star of India)
1306 North Harbor Drive
San Diego, Calif. 92101
Phone (714) 239-0625
Capt. Kenneth Reynard, Fleet Captain

Karl Kortum

Location: The Museum is at the foot of Polk Street and the ships are moored nearby at Pier 43, Fisherman's Wharf.

Vessels: The Balclutha, a typical British merchant ship of the late Victorian period, was launched in Scotland in 1886. She was in commercial service until 1933. Saved from destruction by the Museum in 1954 she has been restored to her original state as a Cape Horn square rigger. A recent addition to the Museum is the sidewheel paddle tug, Eppleton Hall, brought here under her own power from England.

Exhibits: Opened in 1951, the Museum contains a fine collection of maritime artifacts on the nautical history of San Francisco Bay. There are many ship models, photographs, paintings, and portions of vessels. The research library and photograph collection offer a wealth of data for students of maritime research.

Schedule: Daily, 10:00 A. M. to 5:00 P. M.
Ships open 9:00 A. M. to 12:00 P. M.

Admission: Museum: Admission Charge.
Ships: Adults $2.00, Juniors (12-17) $1.00, Children 25c, under 6 free accompanied by parents.

√Refreshments nearby
√Gift Shop
√Limited Free Parking

San Francisco Maritime Museum
Foot of Polk Street
San Francisco, Calif. 94109
Phone (415) 673-0700
Karl Kortum, Director

√Memberships available on request.

S. F. Maritime State Historic Park

Location: The vessels are berthed at the Hyde Street Pier, 2905 Hyde Street, on San Francisco Bay.

Vessels: Five historic craft are at this unique State Historic Park. Four of the vessels have been extensively restored and are open to visitors. The C. A. Thayer is a three-masted lumber schooner. Built in 1895, she served many years in the coastwise lumber trade, and later carried varied cargo until she was retired in 1950. Alma is a scow schooner, a unique type of sailing vessel built for San Francisco Bay service. The Wapama is the last of the steam schooners used in the West Coast lumber trade. Largest member of the fleet is the paddle-wheel, walking beam ferry Eureka, one of the best known of the once numerous Bay ferries. A new addition is the steam tugboat Hercules, built in 1907 and now awaiting restoration. A "By-Word" electronic system enables visitors to hear narration as they view the vessels.

Schedule: Daily, year round, 10:00 A. M. to 5:00 P. M.

Admission: Adults 75c, Children 25c, under 6 free.
School groups 25c per person.

√Refreshments
√Restaurant nearby
√Gift Shop
√City Parking

S. F. Maritime State Historic Park
2905 Hyde Street
San Francisco, Calif. 94109
Phone (415) 441-2116
Harry Dring, Director

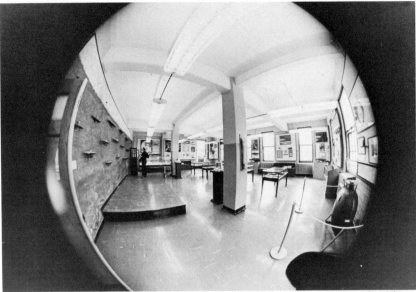

Location: The Museum is in the north end of Building 83 at the Naval Submarine Base in Groton. The Museum can be visited on the Gray Line bus tour of the Base, leaving from the Oasis Restaurant on Route 12 near the main gate.

Exhibits: Initially established in Groton by the Electric Boat Division of General Dynamics Corp., and then donated to the Navy in 1964, the Submarine Force Library and Museum offers a detailed historical record of undersea craft. Of note is a file of 50,000 photographs of submarines and related subjects. There are 50 submarine models ranging from the 54 ft. Holland (SS-1) to modern day nuclear vessels. Other items include paintings, battle flags and pennants and equipment from decommissioned submarines.

Schedule: Monday through Saturday, 10:00 A. M. to 4:00 P. M.
Sundays, 11:00 A. M. to 4:00 P. M.
Gray Line tours run weekends year round, Sat. 10:00 A. M. and 2:00 P. M. Sun. 11:30 A. M. and 2:00 P. M. Daily tours, July-Labor Day, hourly, 10:00 A. M. to 3:00 P. M.

Admission: Free. There is a charge for bus tour.

Note: General visiting of the Base is not allowed. Public access to the Base is by means of Gray Line tour.

√Gift Shop
√Free Parking

Gray Line of New London-Mystic
24 Hamilton Street
New London, Conn. 06320
Phone (203) 443-1831

√Memberships available on request.

Mystic Seaport

Location: The Sabino operates from a dock north of the New York Yacht Club Building on the Mystic Seaport grounds. The boat will operate mostly on the Mystic River.

Vessels: Built in East Boothbay, Maine, in 1908, Sabino spent her initial years in passenger service in the Boothbay Harbor and Kennebec River regions. In 1929 she was sold to the Casco Bay Lines who used her in service out of Portland, Maine, until 1959. After extensive rehabilitation, the 57-ft. long vessel re-entered active service out of Newburyport, Mass. in 1967. In 1973 she began operating in a new location out of Mystic Seaport. In the course of each trip there is an interpretive talk covering the boat's steam plant and the maritime history of the Mystic River area. The Sabino is considered the last coal fired passenger steamboat in regular service in the United States.

Schedule: Daily, Summer. Weekends, Spring and Fall. A number of 35-minute trips are operated in the course of each day. A longer evening run offers a round trip to Noank.

Fare: There is an additional fare for the boat over and above the admission charge to Mystic Seaport, except for the evening run when boat fare only is needed.

Note: Group rate available. Boat is open to public charter.

√Refreshments
√Restaurant
√Gift Shop   Mystic Seaport
√Free Parking
√Picnic Area

Mystic Seaport
Mystic, Conn. 06355
Phone (203) 536-2631
Waldo C. M. Johnston, Director

√Memberships available on request.

10

Mystic Seaport

Location: A short distance south of Interstate 95 on Greenmanville Avenue (Conn. 27) in the old port of Mystic.

Vessels: The wooden whaler, Charles W. Morgan, built in New Bedford, Mass. in 1841 is now a designated National Historic Landmark. The Joseph Conrad, a square-rigged training vessel, was built in Denmark in 1882. The third large ship on display is the Gloucester fishing schooner L. A. Dunton, built in Essex, Mass., 1921.

Exhibits: Mystic Seaport is located on forty acres along the Mystic River. Extensive collections of maritime treasures including ship models, scrimshaw, figureheads and over 200 small craft are on display. Over 40 restored buildings represent a coastal community of the Age of Sail, with many operating craft shops.

Schedule: April 10 - December 1, Daily, 9:00 A. M. to 5:00 P. M. December - April 9, Daily, 10:00 A. M. to 4:00 P. M. Grounds close 3 hours later in Summer. Closed Christmas.

Admission: April 10 - December 1: Adults $4.25, Children $1.75. December - April 9: Adults $3.75, Children $1.50.
Two day ticket available.
Senior citizen and student rates available.
Group rates by advance reservations only.

√Refreshments
√Restaurant
√Gift Shop
√Free Parking
√Picnic Area

Mystic Seaport
Mystic, Conn. 06355
Phone (203) 536-2631
Waldo C. M. Johnston, Director

√Memberships available on request.

11

Location: The Marine Museum is in the Cannonball House on Front Street. Lightship Overfalls is berthed nearby in the Lewes Canal.

Vessels:: Built in 1938 in Bath, Maine, the Overfalls was in service until 1972. The 700-ton vessel is now part of the historic complex of the Lewes Historical Society.

Exhibits: The Cannonball House, still showing traces of the War of 1812, contains a maritime exhibit with items pertaining to the nautical history of Lewes and Delaware Bay. The Burton-Ingram House, the Thompson Country Store, and several other historic buildings are maintained by the Society.

Schedule: Summer months, Daily, 11:00 A. M. to 3:00 P. M.

Admission: Adults $2.00, Children under 10 free.
Admission includes Lightship, Marine Museum and historic buildings.
Group rate available.

Special Events: Antique Flea Market on 1st Saturday in August. Craft exhibitions and summer concerts in August.

√Refreshments
√Gift Shop
√Free Parking
√Picnic Areas nearby

Lewes Historical Society
W 3rd Street
Lewes, Del. 19958
Phone (302) 645-6708
James E. Marvil, M.D., President

√Memberships available on request.

D.C., WASHINGTON
Lightship Chesapeake

Jack Rottier

Location: The ship is docked off East Potomac Park at 1200 Ohio Drive in Washington, D.C.

Vessels: Built in Charleston, S.C. in 1930 for the Lighthouse Service, the ship began her service as LS-116 marking the entrance to Delaware Bay. In 1933 she was transferred to the Chesapeake Bay station where most of her remaining years of active duty were spent. Decommissioned in 1971, the Chesapeake was acquired by the National Park Service.

Exhibits: Administered by the National Capital Parks of the National Park Service, the Chesapeake contains marine exhibits and facilities for the study of marine life and the Potomac River ecology. There is an extensive program for area students.

Schedule: June-September, Tuesday, Thursday, Saturday and Sunday, 1:00 P. M. to 5:00 P. M.
Rest of year, Saturday and Sunday, 1:00 P. M. to 4:00 P. M.
School and Scout groups by appointment.

Admission: Free.

√Free Parking
√Picnic Area

Lightship Chesapeake
1200 Ohio Drive, S.W.
Washington, D.C. 20242
Phone (202) 426-6896
Thomas N. McFadden, Director

Location: In Building 76 of the Washington Navy Yard. Entered
through the main gate at 9th and M streets, S.E.

Exhibits: More than 4,000 artifacts depict two centuries of U.S. naval
history. Included are notable paintings by distinguished American and foreign artists, uniforms, small arms, torpedoes, naval
guns, missiles, and projectiles (such as a Civil War cannon ball
lodged in the sternpost of USS Kearsarge). There are examples
of major weapons up to a 16-inch gun. A submarine room displays historical artifacts and equipment from underseas craft,
and two midget subs from World War II are on exhibit nearby.
Beautifully crafted ship models include several over 25 feet long.
Displays and dioramas depict major naval battles from the Revolutionary War to the present. Artifacts from famous naval
vessels include a heavy timber from frigate Constitution, items
from battleship Maine, and a 12½-ton anchor of aircraft carrier
Enterprise.

Schedule: Weekdays, 9:00 A. M. to 4:00 P. M. Weekends and Holidays, 10:00 A. M. to 5:00 P. M. Closed Thanksgiving, Christmas,
and New Year's Day.

Admission: Free.

Special Events: Spring festival, July 4th display, and Navy Birthday in
October. Bicentennial exhibits during 1976.

√Refreshments nearby
√Gift Shop
√Free Parking
√Picnic Area

Navy Memorial Museum
Building 76
Washington Navy Yard
Washington, D.C. 20374
Phone (202) 433-2651
Capt. Roger Pineau, USNR, Director

Smithsonian Institution

Location: The exhibits are in the National Museum of History and Technology, situated on Constitution Avenue at 14th Street, next to the Mall in Washington, D.C.

Vessels: The Gunboat Philadelphia was built in 1776 and sunk at the Battle of Valcour Island on Lake Champlain. Raised in 1935, the vessel is now on display in the Armed Forces Hall.

Exhibits: There are two exhibit areas of nautical interest at the Smithsonian. The Hall of American Merchant Marine features a collection of over 175 of the world's finest ship models. Here one can see the evolution of American shipping from colonial times to the 20th Century. The Armed Forces Hall displays models of fighting ships as well as collections of naval arms, uniforms and other memorabilia.

Schedule: April - Labor Day, 10:00 A. M. to 9:00 P. M.
Sept. 4 - March 31, 10:00 A. M. to 5:30 P. M.
Open every day of the year except Christmas.

Admission: Free.

√Refreshments
√Restaurant
√Gift Shop
√City Parking
√Picnic Area

National Museum of History and Technology
Smithsonian Institution
Washington, D.C. 20560
Phone (202) 381-6277
Philip K. Lundberg, Curator Naval History

Naval Historical Foundation

Location: At 1610 H Street, N. W., just off historic Lafayette Square.

Exhibits: Opened in 1950, the Museum is located in the carriage house adjoining the historic home of Stephen Decatur, who distinguished himself in the Tripolitan War. It is also named for Commodore Thomas Truxtun, another naval figure of the period. Sponsored by the Naval Historical Foundation, the exhibits cover the Merchant Marine, U.S. Marine Corps, and Coast Guard in addition to the U.S. Navy. Displays are changed periodically. The current exhibit depicts the Bicentennial theme "Men Who Made the Navy," displaying the contributions made in 200 years of naval science. Much of the Foundation's extensive collection of naval items is kept at the Library of Congress.

Schedule: Daily, year round, 10:30 A. M. to 4:00 P. M. Closed Holidays.

Admission: Free.

√Gift Shop

√City Parking

Truxtun-Decatur Naval Museum
c/o Naval Historical Foundation
Room 218 Building 220, Navy Yard
Washington, D.C. 20374
Phone (202) ST 3-2573
Vice Adm. W. S. DeLany, U.S.N. (ret.) President

√Memberships available on request.

16

Location: The ship is berthed at the Vinoy Basin next to the Municipal Pier at 345 Second Ave. N.E. in St. Petersburg.

Vessels: The Bounty was built in Lunenburg, Nova Scotia following
plans of the original ship of 1787. Completed in 1960, she is
118 ft. long and of 30-ft. 6-inch beam. The 480-ton vessel sailed
to Tahiti for use in the film "Mutiny On The Bounty". Afterwards
the Bounty made an extensive trip to U.S. and European ports.
In 1965, after a year at the New York World's Fair she sailed to
St. Petersburg to go on public exhibit. Visitors can see furnishings and nautical items laid out as though Bligh's crew had
just left the ship. On shore a Tahitian village surrounds a replica
of the long boat on which Capt. Bligh sailed 3,600 miles after
the mutiny in 1789.

Schedule: Daily, year round, 9:00 A. M. to 10:00 P. M.

Admission: Adults $2.00, Children (4-12) 75c, under 4 free.
Group rates available.

√Refreshments
√Gift Shop
√Free Parking

MGM's Bounty Exhibit
345 Second Ave., N.E.
St. Petersburg, Fla. 33701
Phone (813) 896-3117
Hugh Boyd, Director

Confederate Naval Museum

Location: At 101 4th Street, just west of U.S. 27 in Columbus.

Vessels: The remains of the 225-ft. ironclad ram CSS Muscogee and the 130-ft. wooden gunboat CSS Chattahoochee are on exhibit. Both vessels were built in the area during the Civil War, burned and sunk in April 1865 and raised from the Chattahoochee River during the Civil War Centennial.

Exhibits: Under the management of the U.S. Bicentennial Trust Fund, Columbus, Georgia; the Museum contains dioramas, interpretive exhibits and relics of the Confederate Navy. On display are artifacts recovered from the two Confederate vessels at the Museum.

Schedule: Tuesday through Saturday, 10:00 A. M. to 5:00 P. M. Sundays, 2:00 P. M. to 5:00 P. M. Closed Mondays.

Admission: Free.

√Gift Shop
√Free Parking

Confederate Naval Museum
P.O. Box 1022
Columbus, Ga. 31902
Phone (404) 327-9798
Robert Holcombe, Curator

Location: At 503 E. River Street on the historic waterfront of Savannah.

Vessels: The Ships of the Sea Museum is housed in an old warehouse dating to 1898. Of particular interest is the fine display of ship models. Over 150 miniature vessels cover nautical history from Columbus to the nuclear ship Savannah. There is a collection of ships in bottles by Peter Barlow, a well-known English craftsman. These ships are considered one of the finest assemblies of this type of work in existence. Two exhibit floors contain a full sized ships chandlery, a carpenter shop and an exhibit gallery. The extensive collection of maritime artifacts includes marine paintings and pictures, figureheads, scrimshaw, ship's furniture and naval arms.

Schedule: Daily, year round, 10:00 A. M. to 5:00 P. M.

Admission: Adults $1.00, Children 50c, under 7 free.
Group rate available.

Special Events: Special exhibits scheduled during the year in the new gallery.

√Refreshments
√Gift Shop
√Free Parking

Ships of the Sea Museum
503 E. River Street
Savannah, Ga. 31401
Phone (912) 232-1511
Joseph H. Moore, Director

Hawaii Visitors Bureau

Location: The ship is berthed at Pier 5, Honolulu Harbor, just off Ala Moana Boulevard.

Vessels: Built in Scotland in 1878, the Falls of Clyde first served as a general cargo vessel under the British flag. In 1898 she was bought by Capt. William Matson and was one of the first ships of the Matson Line. Converted to an oil tanker in 1907 she was in service until 1958. Bought by the people of Hawaii through public subscription in 1963, ownership and restoration was assumed by the Bishop Museum in 1968. The Falls of Clyde is now undergoing extensive restoration to her old outward appearance as a full-rigged ship.

Schedule: Daily, year round, 10:00 A. M. to 11:00 P. M.

Admission: Adults $1.50, Military (active duty) $1.00, Children to 17, 50c, under 7 free.

√Gift Shop in RR car
√Metered Parking

The Falls of Clyde
Pier 5
Honolulu, Hawaii 96819
Phone (808) 531-5439

U. S. Navy

Location: At the Naval Submarine Base in Pearl Harbor.

Exhibits: Opened in 1970, the Pacific Submarine Museum shows the history of undersea craft from the Navy's first submarine, the USS Holland, to the nuclear powered vessels of the present. There are numerous documents and photographs as well as much sub memorabilia. An operating periscope is an interesting feature of the Museum. A movie theater features films on submarine activities. Outside the main building one can see the conning tower of the USS Parche, a Submarine Memorial and a display of torpedoes. The research library contains numerous documents on submarine war activities and books and periodicals about submarines.

Schedule: Wednesday through Sunday, 9:30 A. M. to 5:00 P. M.

Admission: Free.

√Refreshments nearby
√Free Parking

Pacific Submarine Museum
Naval Submarine Base
FPO, San Francisco, Calif. 96610
Phone (808) 471-0632
Karen A. Pritchard, Curator

21

Location: At 57th Street and Lake Shore Drive in Jackson Park, Chicago.

Vessels: The German submarine U-505, captured during World War II, is on display alongside the main building. Conducted tours through the undersea vessel are followed by official films of the 1944 capture.

Exhibits: Highlighting the nautical exhibits are a life size replica of the USS Constitution gun deck, a mizzenmast deck of a Yankee windjammer and a submarine conning tower. The ship model collection contains 65 scale models ranging from an Egyptian Nile boat of 2750 B.C. to a Great Lakes ore carrier of 1960. Other exhibits relate to weather forecasting, naval aviation, and atomic seapower.

Schedule: Daily, May 1-Labor Day, 9:30 A. M. to 5:30 P. M. Rest of year closes at 4:00 P. M. on weekdays and 5:30 P. M. on weekends and holidays. Closed Christmas.

Admission: Free.

√Refreshments
√Gift Shop
√Cafeteria

Museum of Science & Industry
57th Street and Lake Shore Drive
Chicago, Ill. 60637
Phone (312) 684-1414
Dr. Victor Danilov, Director

Photo by Talbot

Location: The Keokuk River Museum is situated at the foot of Main Street in Victory Park, on the banks of the Mississippi River.

Vessels: The George M. Verity was built by the Dubuque Boat and Boiler Works in 1927 for the Upper Mississippi Barge Line Company. Under her original name, the S.S. Thorpe, she operated on both the upper and lower Mississippi until 1940, when she was sold to the Armco Steel Corp. and rechristened the George M. Verity. The Verity towed coal barges on the Ohio River until 1960, when she was donated to the town of Keokuk for a river museum where visitors can examine a typical Mississippi River sternwheel towboat.

Schedule: Mid-April to November 1, Monday through Saturday, 9:00 A. M. to 5:00 P. M. and Sundays and Holidays, 10:00 A. M. to 6:00 P. M.

Admission: Adults 75c, Children 40c, under 6 free.
Group rate available.

√Refreshments
√Gift Shop
√Free Parking
√Picnic Area

William L. Talbot, Chairman
Keokuk River Commission
226 High St.
Keokuk, Iowa 52632
Phone (319) 524-4765

Lin Caufield

Location: Boat departs from wharf at the foot of Fourth Street in downtown Louisville.

Vessels: Built in 1914, The Belle of Louisville has had a varied career on the inland rivers. She has served as packet boat, ferry and excursion boat. By the late 1950's she was retired from active service and allowed to fall into a state of disrepair. Purchased in 1962 by Jefferson County, the Belle has been completely refurbished and is now operated by the Belle of Louisville Operating Board, a joint city and county agency. With her steam whistle, calliope and stern wheel, a trip on the Belle recaptures the romance of the steamboat era.

Schedule: Memorial Day through Labor Day. Trips daily except Monday at 2:00 P. M. (boarding and ticket sales start at 1:00 P. M.) Saturday evening dance cruise at 8:00 P. M. and special trips on Holidays.

Fare: Adults $2.00, Children (under 12) $1.00.
Saturday Eve.: Adults $4.00.
Charter rates available.

Special Events: Annual Steamboat Race every May between the Delta Queen and the Belle of Louisville.

√Refreshments on boat

Steamer Belle of Louisville
Foot of Fourth Street
Louisville, Ky. 40202
Phone (502) 582-2547

24

Location: The Museum consists of four sites along the Kennebec River in the historic shipbuilding city of Bath. The Museum includes exhibits and displays at the Sewall Mansion, the Percy and Small Shipyard, the Apprenticeshop, and the Winter Street Center.

Exhibits: The Bath Marine Museum commemorates 365 years of Maine maritime history in a city itself an example of the living heritage of the past. Four sites offer displays of marine artifacts and live exhibits of shipbuilding techniques. Included are ship models, navigation instruments, seamen's crafts and scrimshaw, and the work of noted marine artists. At the Percy and Small Shipyard the original buildings are being restored and vessels are under construction. During the summer season a boat service connects Percy and Small Shipyard with the other museum sites.

Schedule: May 22 - Oct. 17, Daily, 10:00 A. M. to 5:00 P. M.

Admission: Summer season (includes boat ride): Adults $3.50, Children $1.00. Spring and Fall seasons: Adults $2.75, Children 75c. Note: If one does not have time to enjoy all of the museum facilities in one day, tickets can be validated at the admissions desk for a "Second Day" pass.

√Please Touch Children's Exhibits
√Gift Shop
√Free Parking
√Picnic Area

Marine Research Society of Bath
Headquarters: 963 Washington Street
Bath, Maine 04530
Phone (207) 443-6311
Ralph L. Snow, Executive Director

√Memberships available on request

Location: The Museum is situated at 100 Commercial Street in the picturesque town of Boothbay Harbor on the coast of Maine.

Vessels: A recent addition to the many attractions in Boothbay, the Sherman Zwicker is a typical Grand Banks fishing schooner. The 180-ton vessel was built by Smith & Rhuland in 1941 and has a diesel engine for power. Until her arrival in Boothbay she served as one of many ships used for fishing on the historic Grand Banks. Aboard the Sherman Zwicker are exhibits on nautical subjects and fishing.

Schedule: Weekends, Memorial Day through mid- June. Daily, mid-June through September 15.
Open 10:00 A. M. to 5:00 P. M. except during July and August when hours are from 9:00 A. M. to 9:00 P. M.

Admission: Adults $1.00, Children 50c, under 2 free.
Group rate available.

Special Events: Annual "Windjammer Days" during the second week of July.

√Gift Shop
√Free Parking

Grand Banks Schooner Museum
100 Commercial Street
Boothbay Harbor, Maine 04538
Phone (207) 633-5603
George H. McEvoy, Director

Photo by Frank Claes

Location: Within view of Penobscot Bay on the corner of Route 1 and Church Street in the Village of Searsport about 20 miles south of Bangor.

Exhibits: At the Penobscot Marine Museum the visitor can share in the knowledge of the life and achievements of seafaring men who developed the 19th Century maritime history of Penobscot Bay as well as other coastal areas of Maine. Six buildings contain exhibits that include an extensive collection of marine paintings and prints, furnishings from the homes of Searsport shipmasters, shipibuildinig tools, navigational instruments and charts, and other nautical memorabilia. There are numerous models of Maine built vessels as well as builders half-models.

Schedule: Daily, June through September. Monday through Saturday, 9:00 A. M. to 5:00 P. M. Sundays, 1:00 P. M. to 5:00 P. M.

Admission: Adults $2.00, Children (6-11) 50c, under 6 free. Group rate available. Advance reservations requested.

√Gift Shop
√Free Parking

Penobscot Marine Museum
Searsport, Maine 04974
Phone (207) 548-6634
Richard V. Palmer, Director

MARYLAND, ANNAPOLIS **Nautical Museum**
Annapolis Naval Historical Wax Museum

Al Peabody

Location: At the City Dock in downtown Annapolis. The Museum is two blocks from the Naval Academy.

Exhibits: The Annapolis Naval Historical Wax Museum dramatizes the history of Colonial Maryland and the U.S. Navy. There are 31 scenes with a total of 150 life-size figures. A number of the scenes employ sound and light effects. The history of the U.S. Navy is represented from John Paul Jones in 1775 to John F. Kennedy on board P. T. 109. Other naval heroes shown include Stephen Decatur, James Lawrence, Admiral David Porter and Admiral William F. Halsey.

Schedule: Daily, year round, November through April, 10:00 A. M. to 6:00 P. M. May through October, 9:00 A. M. to 9:00 P. M.

Admission: Adults $2.00, Children (under 12) $1.00, under 6 free. Group rates available.

√Metered Parking
√Gift Shop

Annapolis Naval Historical Wax Museum
110 Dock Street
Annapolis, Md. 21401
Phone (301) 268-7727
Alice Weathersbee, Director

28

U. S. Naval Academy Museum

Location: The Museum is located in Preble Hall near Gate 3 of the Academy at Hanover Street and Maryland Avenue in Annapolis.

Exhibits: In 1849, four years after the Naval Academy opened, the historical collection was started. Through the years nautical items have been continually added, so that at present over 55,000 objects are contained in the Museum. Featured are over 250 fine ship models. The world's largest collection of items relating to John Paul Jones is housed here. Exhibited is the famous flag from the Battle of Lake Erie with the words 'Don't Give Up the Ship.'

Schedule: Tuesday-Saturday, 9:00 A. M. to 5:00 P. M. Sundays, 11:00 A. M. to 5:00 P. M. Closed Mondays, Thanksgiving, Christmas and New Years Day.

Admission: Free.

Special Events: Special exhibitions are held at the Museum during the year.

√Naval Inst. Bookshop   U.S. Naval Academy Museum
 in Preble Hall   Annapolis, Md. 21402
          Phone (301) 267-2108
          Dr. W. W. Jeffries, Director

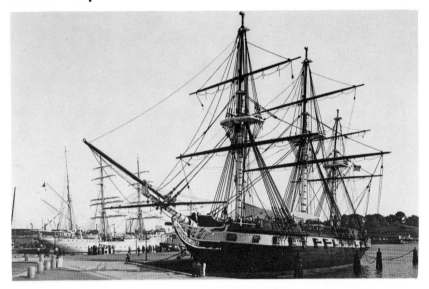

Location: The vessels are berthed at the Constellation Dock at Pratt and Light Streets in downtown Baltimore.

Vessels: Four ships make up the Baltimore Seaport fleet. The Frigate Constellation, a registered historic shrine, is the oldest ship in the world continuously afloat. Commissioned in 1797, she has participated in every American war except the Revolution and the Vietnamese conflict. Many interesting displays are aboard, including early Navy relics and the memorabilia of Commodore Charles Stewart. The Submarine U.S.S. Torsk (SS-423) served in the Pacific and sank the last 4 Japanese ships in WW II. The Lightship Five Fathoms, veteran of 50 years service off Cape May is a recent addition to the Baltimore Seaport. The latest vessel to arrive is the schooner Freedom, former Naval Academy training ship.

Schedule: June 19 through Labor Day, Daily, 10:00 A.M. to 6:00 P.M. Rest of year, Monday through Saturday, 10:00 A. M. to 4:00 P. M. Sundays, Noon to 5:00 P. M.

Admission: Admission to each vessel: Adults $1.00, Children 50c, under 6 free.
Group rates available upon advance notice.

Special Events: Cannons aboard the Constellation are fired on Sundays during the summer.

√Restaurants nearby
√Gift Shop
√Free Parking

Baltimore Seaport
Constellation Dock
Baltimore, Md. 21202
Phone (301) 539-1797

C. C. *Harris*

Location: Navy Point in the historic town of St. Michaels overlooking the Miles River. Reached by and via Md. Rte. 33.

Vessels: J. T. Leonard, 1882 gaffed-rigged oyster sloop.
Edna E. Lockwood, 1889 log-built bugeye.
Rosie Parks, Skipjack.

Exhibits: Oriented to Chesapeake Bay maritime history, the Museum exhibits ship models, small boats, paintings, antique marine engines, navigation instruments and a waterfowling exhibit. There are ten buildings including the Hooper Strait Lighthouse on the 5-acre waterfront site. The Museum library and maintenance shops are located a short distance from main grounds.

Schedule: May-October, Daily, 10:00 A. M. to 5:00 P. M.
November-April, 10:00 A. M. to 4:00 P. M.
Closed Christmas Day and non-holiday Mondays during winter schedule.

Admission: Adults $2.00, Children (6-16) 75c, under 6 free if with adult. Group rate available with confirmed reservation.

√Docking Facilities
√Gift Shop
√Free Parking
√Picnic Area

Chesapeake Bay Maritime Museum
P.O. Box 636
St. Michaels, Md. 21663
Phone (301) 745-2916
R. J. Holt, Director

√Memberships available on request.

Boston Tea Party Ship

Location: The ship and museum are at the Congress Street Bridge, close to downtown Boston. The original Tea Party site, 2 blocks away near Atlantic Avenue, was filled in long ago and is now high and dry.

Vessels: The Brig Beaver II is a full-size working replica of one of the three original Tea Party ships. The 112-foot brigantine, rebuilt from an old Danish trading schooner, sailed across the Atlantic with a cargo of tea and was the scene of the recent Bicentennial Tea Party Celebration.

Exhibits: Commemorating the event of Dec. 16, 1773, the Tea Party Museum houses an audio-visual presentation on the Tea Party, its causes, and its effect on the growing resistance of the Colonials to British rule. Exhibits portray the political and economic conditions of the time in Boston. There are a number of artifacts relating to the Tea Party including a chest believed to have been thrown overboard during the historic event.

Schedule: Daily, May through September, 9:00 A. M. to 8:00 P. M. Rest of year closes at 5:00 P. M.

Admission: Adults $1.50, Children 75c, under 5 free. Group rates available.

√Refreshments
√Gift Shop
√City Parking

Boston Tea Party Ship
Congress Street Bridge
Boston, Mass. 02210
Phone (617) 338-1773
Maureen Charbonneau, Director

Museum of Science

Location: At Science Park on the Charles River Bridge between Leverett Circle and Lechmere Square, close to downtown Boston.

Exhibits: Among its many collections, the Museum of Science contains an extensive maritime exhibit. Fifteen fine ship models range from an ancient Egyptian seagoing craft to modern vessels. One of the Museum's miniature dioramas on New England industry portrays the famed McKay Shipyard of East Boston. A revolving Fresnel lens from a lighthouse in New Jersey is another display of note.

Schedule: Daily, year round, Monday - Saturday, 10:00 A. M. to 5:00 P. M. Friday night until 10:00 P. M. Sundays, 11:00 A. M. to 5:00 P. M. Closed Thanksgiving, Christmas, New Year's Day.

Admission: Adults $2.50, Children (5-16) and students, senior citizens and active duty servicemen $1.50, under 5 free.
Group rates available.
(Additional charge for Hayden Planetarium.)

√Refreshments   Museum of Science
√Restaurant   Science Park
√Gift Shop   Boston, Mass. 02114
√Parking Nominal Rates   Phone (617) 723-2500
                                  Bradford Washburn, Director

√Memberships available on request.

Location: The U.S.S. Constitution is berthed in the Boston Historical Park at Wapping and Chelsea Streets in Charlestown.

Vessels: Launched in Boston in 1797, the Constitution carried 54 guns and a crew of 475. During 1803-1805 she served in the Tripolitan War, which ended with the signing of the peace treaty in her cabin on June 3, 1805. Following her famous defeat of the Guerriere in the War of 1812, she was fondly called "Old Ironsides". The Constitution is the only frigate still surviving perfectly preserved and fully commissioned in the U.S. Navy, and is the Flagship of the Commandant, First Naval District. Constitution was reopened to visitors in March 1975 after an extensive renovation, the first phase of which continues until the end of June 1976. An adjacent museum devoted to the history of the vessel and displaying artifacts and memorabilia will open in April 1976.

Schedule: Daily, year round, 9:30 A. M. to 4:00 P. M.

Admission: Free.

√Refreshments
√Gift Shop
√Free Parking

Commanding Officer, U.S.S. Constitution
Boston, Mass. 02129
Phone (617) 242-0144
Cdr. Tyrone G. Martin, USN, Comm. Officer

Hart Nautical Museum

Location: The Hart Museum is at 55 Massachusetts Avenue (M.I.T. Building 5) in Cambridge, across the Charles River from Boston.

Exhibits: This fine display of nautical items is under the jurisdiction of the Massachusetts Institute of Technology's Department of Ocean Engineering. The Museum was established to show ship and marine engineering developments to M.I.T. students. On display are numerous rigged models of merchant and war ships ranging from early sailing craft to present day vessels and half models of yachts and merchant ships from about 1850 and marine engine models.

Schedule: Daily, year round, 9:00 A. M. to 9:00 P. M. Evenings, weekends and holidays use entrance at 77 Massachusetts Avenue.

Admission: Free.

√City Parking   Hart Nautical Museum
                                 55 Massachusetts Avenue
                                 Cambridge, Mass. 02139
                                 Phone (617) 253-5942 (Tuesday-Thursday)
                                 William A. Baker, Director

Photo by Mason Mayhew

Location: At Cooke and School Streets in Edgartown, an historic whaling port, on Martha's Vineyard island. Ferry service runs to Edgartown from Woods Hole on Cape Cod.

Exhibits: The Dukes County Historical Society, founded in 1922, has assembled a large collection of nautical items and local memorabilia. The Thomas Cooke House built in 1765 contains exhibits of scrimshaw, whaling implements, ship models and pictures. A lighthouse tower is topped by the Fresnel lens and mechanism of the historic Gay Head Lighthouse. An adjoining boat shed holds a whale boat and maritime relics. A research library has many works on nautical subjects. A full-size replica of the try-works of a whale ship is another exhibit of interest.

Schedule: June 15 through October 15, Tuesday through Saturday, 10:00 A. M. to 4:30 P. M. Closed Sundays and Holidays. Winter Schedule (library only), Thursday & Friday, 1:00 P. M. to 4:00 P. M. Saturdays, 10:00 A. M. to Noon and 1:00 P. M. to 4:00 P. M. Museum open other times by appointment for groups.

Admission: Adults $1.00, Children 50c, infants free.

√Book Shop
√Free Parking

Dukes County Historical Society
P.O. Box 827
Edgartown, Mass., 02539
Phone (617) 627-4441
Thomas Norton, Curator

√Memberships available on request.

Alban J. Bernier

Location: The museum is situated at 70 Water Street in Fall River. It is only a short distance from Battleship Cove and the U.S.S. Massachusetts.

Exhibits: Featured in this fine museum is a large collection of prints, paintings, and broadsides, covering the growth of marine steam-power from the time of Robert Fulton to the present day. Over 65 models are on display, many from the famous Seamens Church Institute collection. There is an outstanding exhibit of Fall River Line items including numerous photographs and much memorabilia such as furnishings, uniform parts and crockery. Other exhibits include knot tying and nautical crafts.

Schedule: Monday-Friday, 9:00 A. M. to 5:00 P. M.
    Saturdays, Sundays and Holidays, Noon to 5:00 P. M.

Admission: Adults $1.25, Children 75c, under 3 free.

Special Events: Fall River Line Day, May 19, 1975.

√Gift Shop   The Marine Museum at Fall River, Inc.
√Free Parking   P.O. Box 1147
                       Fall River, Mass. 02722
                       Phone (617) 674-3533
        √Memberships available on request.

Location: The U.S.S. Massachusetts, Destroyer Kennedy and Sub Lionfish are berthed at Battleship Cove in Fall River. From I-195, use exit 11, and follow signs.

Vessels: The Battleship Massachusetts (BB-59) made her last voyage in June 1965 when she entered the harbor at Fall River to become a memorial to those who gave their lives in the service of their country in World War II. The 35,000 ton ship was completed in 1942 at the Fall River Shipyard in Quincy, Mass. War service included 35 major naval engagements and the earning of 11 battle stars. The Lionfish (SS-198) is a typical World War II attack submarine. The Destroyer Joseph P. Kennedy, Jr. is a World War II type vessel modernized for anti-submarine warfare. A new addition is a P.T. boat (PT-796). A complete tour of the vessels, augmented by a sound system on the Battleship, takes about 2½ hours.

Schedule: Daily, year round, 9:00 A. M. to 5:00 P. M.
Closed Thanksgiving and Christmas Day.

Admission: For all ships: Adults $3.00, Children $1.25, Tots 50c, under 2 free.

Special Events: VJ Day Ceremonies held on board Battleship on August 14.

√Refreshments   U.S.S. Massachusetts Memorial Comm., Inc.
√Gift Shop   Battleship Cove
√Free Parking   Fall River, Mass. 02721
√Picnic Area   Phone (617) 678-1100
                              Paul S. Vaitses, Jr., Exec. Director
              √Memberships available on request.

MASSACHUSETTS, MILTON
Museum of the American China Trade

Nautical Museum

Photo by George M. Cushing

Location: At 215 Adams Street in Milton, a few miles south of downtown Boston.

Exhibits: The Museum of the American China Trade focuses upon one of the most significant aspects of the American experience from the Colonial period to the end of the age of sail. The 1833 Capt. Robert Bennet Forbes House, a National Historic Landmark, contains an extensive collection of China Trade art objects, memorabilia and documents pertaining to the maritime commerce with the Orient. The exhibits at the Museum describe and interpret the substance and nature of the China Trade. Porcelain, textiles, teas and spices constitute a visual presentation of the objects of the trade. Paintings and portraits recall the ports, the ships in use and the men that sailed them.

Schedule: Tuesday through Saturday, 2:00 P. M. to 5:00 P. M. Closed Holidays.

Admission: Adults $1.50, Children 50c.

√Gift Shop
√Free Parking
√Picnic Area

Museum of the American China Trade
215 Adams Street
Milton, Mass. 02186
Phone (617) 696--1815
Paul E. Molitor, Jr., Director

√Memberships available on request.

Photo by Bill Haddon

Location: The Whaling Museum is at the head of Steamboat Wharf in historic Nantucket.

Exhibits: Nantucket was a leading whaling port until about 100 years ago. This nautical collection, housed in the old Brick Candlehouse built in 1847, preserves the historical heritage of the whaling era. The Museum features an extensive display of whaling memorabilia, including tools, try works, log books, prints and portraits. There are exhibits on whaling crafts, such as a sail loft, rigging loft, shipsmith's shop. The collection of scrimshaw features over 1,600 pieces. The Nantucket Historical Association sponsors the Whaling Museum and maintains several other historic buildings nearby.

Schedule: Daily, end of May to mid-October, 10:00 A. M. to 5:00 P.M.

Admission: Adults $1.25, Children 60c, under 5 free.
        Group rate available.

√Free Parking   Nantucket Historical Assoc.
√Limited Gift Shop   Box 1016
                                       Nantucket, Mass. 02554
                                       Phone (617) 228-1894
                                       Leroy H. True, Administrator
        √Memberships available on request.

Photo by Norman Fortier

Location: The Whaling Museum is at 18 Johnny Cake Hill in New Bedford.

Exhibits: Sponsored by the Old Dartmouth Historical Society, The Whaling Museum is America's largest museum in its field. Of particular interest is the half-scale model of the Bark Lagoda typical of the whaleships which sailed out of New Bedford around 1850. Nearly 60 ft. in length, it is the world's largest ship model. On display are fine collections of scrimshaw, marine carvings, paintings, and whaling tools.

Schedule: June 1 - Sept. 30 open Daily 9:00 A. M. to 5:00 P. M. Sundays, 1:00 P. M. - 5:00 P. M.
Oct. 1 - May 31 open daily except Mondays, 9 A. M. to 5:00 P. M., Sundays, 1:00 P. M. to 5:00 P. M.

Admission: Adults $1.50, Children 75c, under 6 free.
Group rate available.

√Gift Shop
√Free Parking

The Whaling Museum
18 Johnny Cake Hill
New Bedford, Mass. 02740
Phone (617) 997-0046
Richard C. Kugler, Director

Plimoth Plantation

Location: Berthed at State Pier in Plymouth, just off the intersection of North and Water Streets close to famous Plymouth Rock.

Vessels: The Mayflower II is a full-scale re-creation of the ship which brought the Pilgrims to America in 1620. Exhibits aboard show what life was like on that historic 66-day voyage on a vessel crowded with 102 passengers, about 25 crewmen and all the supplies needed to sustain the new colony. The Mayflower II is owned and operated by Plimoth Plantation, a non-profit educational institution, operators of a re-creation of the Pilgrim settlement three miles south of Plymouth Rock. The vessel is 104 ft. long with a gross tonnage of 181 tons. Built in England, the vessel sailed across the Atlantic in 1957 with a crew of 33 men under the command of Captain Alan Villiers.

Schedule: April-November, Daily, 9:00 A. M. to 5:00 P. M., except during July and August when tickets will be sold until 8:00 P. M.

Admission: Adults $1.25, Children 60c, under 5 free.

√City Parking

Mayflower II
P.O. Box 1620
Plymouth, Mass. 02360
Phone (617) 746-1622
David B. Freeman, Director

√Memberships available on request.

Peabody Museum

Location: At 161 Essex Street in the historic port of Salem.

Exhibits: Dating back to the East India Marine Society organized in 1799, the Peabody Museum is located in the East India Marine Hall built in 1824. In 1867 the Museum was renamed for one of its benefactors, George Peabody. The exhibits are arranged in three groups: ethnology, natural history, and maritime history. The nautical display features a very large collection of ship models. There is a full-size reconstruction of rooms from the yacht Cleopatra's Barge, built in 1816. Exhibits of nautical instruments, shipbuilders tools, paintings and photographs can be seen. A comprehensive library and large study collection of nautical material is available to qualified persons. A new East Wing of the Museum opens in the Spring of 1976.

Schedule: Daily, Monday through Saturday, 9:00 A. M. to 5:00 P. M., Sundays and Holidays, 1:00 P. M. to 5:00 P. M. Closed Thanksgiving, Christmas and New Year's Day.

Admission: Adults $1.50, Children 75c, under 6 free.
Group rate available.

√Gift Shop
√City Parking

Peabody Museum of Salem
161 Essex Street
Salem, Mass. 01970
Phone (617) 745-9500
Ernest S. Dodge, Director

√Memberships available on request.

43

Kendall Whaling Museum

Location: At 27 Everett Street in Sharon, about 20 miles south of Boston. From Route 27 in Sharon, take Upland Road to Everett Street.

Exhibits: The Kendall Whaling Museum exhibits a large collection of material relating to the whaling industry and its rise and fall. Of note is the large number of paintings and prints not only from the United States but also from other deep-sea whaling nations of the past; Japan, Britain, Holland and other countries. There are displays of ship models, scrimshaw, whaling artifacts and gear and tools used for whaling. A whaleboat complete with harpoons and gear is on exhibit. Logbooks of whaling vessels and manuscripts relating to the industry can be seen at the Museum.

Schedule: Open weekdays, year round, 10:00 A. M. to 4:00 P. M. Closed weekends and holidays. Group tours by appointment.

Admission: Adults 50c, Children 25c.

√Gift Shop
√Free Parking

Kendall Whaling Museum
P.O. Box 297
Sharon, Mass. 02067
Phone (617) 784-5642
Dr. Kenneth Martin, Director

Location: The Museum entrance is ½ mile south of U.S. 12 between Southfield Rd. and Oakwood Blvd. in Dearborn.

Vessels: The Steamboat Suwanee plies the waters of the lagoon at Greenfield Village. The original Suwanee was a favorite of Thomas Edison on his Florida fishing trips. The present stern-wheeler was constructed in 1930 and is powered with engines built in 1888.

Exhibits: The Henry Ford Museum contains many items of nautical interest. There are exhibits of small craft and marine engines, both steam and internal combustion. Numerous examples of maritime folk art are displayed.

Schedule: Museum and Village: Daily, year round, 9:00 A. M. to 6:00 P. M., except closes at 5:00 P. M., weekdays September, mid-June. Closed Christmas, Thanksgiving, New Year's Day. Suwanee: Daily, June-August. Week-ends, May, September, October.

Admission: Village: Adults $3.00, Children (6-12) $1.25, under 6 free Museum: Same as Village.
Steamboat Suwanee: Additional Charge.

Special Events: Many interesting events are scheduled during the year.

√Refreshments
√Restaurant
√Gift Shop
√Free Parking
√Picnic Area

Greenfield Village & Henry Ford Museum
Dearborn, Mich. 48121
Phone (313) 271-1620
Donald Shelley, President

√Memberships available on request.

45

Dossin Great Lakes Museum

Location: At Belle Isle Park in the middle of the Detroit River. The MacArthur Bridge leads from downtown Detroit to the Island.

Vessels: The maritime history of the Great Lakes is covered extensively in this fine museum. The ship model display is considered the world's largest collection built to a uniform scale. A featured exhibit is the Gothic Room, an elaborately decorated area, once a smoking lounge from the steamer Detroit III. A reconstructed ships bridge overlooks the Detroit River. The record breaking hydroplane Miss Pepsi is on display in one wing of the museum. Other exhibits include marine paintings, navigational equipment, and nautical relics. The Museum is a branch of the Detroit Historical Museum and is assisted by the Great Lakes Maritime Institute.

Schedule: Wednesday through Sunday, year round, 10:00 A. M. to 5:45 P. M.
Closed all National Legal Holidays.

Admission: Suggested Donation: Adults 50c, Children 25c.

√Gift Shop   Dossin Great Lakes Museum
√Free Parking   Strand Drive, Belle Isle
                                    Detroit, Mich. 48207
                                    Phone (313) 824-3157
        √Memberships available on request.

46

MICHIGAN, DOUGLAS
Saugatuck Marine Museum

Steamship

Penrod/Hiawatha

Location: At the foot of Hamilton Street in Douglas, just off Interstate 196 about 10 miles south of Holland.

Vessels: The S.S. Keewatin was built in 1907 in Scotland together with its sister ship the Assiniboia. The ship was floated in two sections from Montreal to Buffalo in order to reach the Great Lakes. In 1908 she began service for the Canadian Pacific Ry. from the Georgian Bay area to the Lakehead cities of Port Arthur and Fort William (now combined as Thunder Bay). The coal-burning vessel was on this route until retired in 1965. In June 1967 the ship was towed to its present berth at the Tower Marina off Lake Michigan. The 350 ft. vessel contains interesting exhibits on the maritime history of the Great Lakes. Alongside is the Reiss, a 60-year-old steam tugboat.

Schedule: Daily, May 1 to October 1. Open from 10:00 A. M. to 4:30 P. M.
Guided tours available.

Admission: Adults $1.00, Children 50c, under 6 free.
Group rate available.
(Rates subject to change).

√Gift Shop
√Free Parking
√Marina

Saugatuck Marine Museum
P.O. Box 436
Douglas, Mich. 49406
Phone (616) 857-2158
Roland J. Peterson, Director

Mackinac Island State Park Commission

Location: Within Ft. Michilimackinac Historic Park at Straits Avenue in Mackinaw City near the Mackinac Bridge.

Exhibits: Open to the public for the first time in 1972, the Mackinac Maritime Park is centered around the old Mackinac Point Lighthouse, built in 1892. The Lighthouse was in service until 1957, when the completion of the Mackinac Bridge reduced the need for its services. The focus of the Park is the maritime history of the region. Within the Lighthouse and its adjoining lightkeepers quarters are exhibits of pictures, models and other nautical items. A closed-circuit T.V. camera is mounted in the tower to show an elevated view of the Straits of Mackinac. The site is a Registered National Historic Landmark, administered by the Mackinac Island State Park Commission as part of Ft. Michilimackinac Historical Park. A replica of the 1775 sloop Welcome, built here during the Revolution, can be seen under construction at the Park.

Schedule: Daily, mid-May - October 15, 9:00 A. M. to 5:00 P. M.

Admission: Adults $2.00, Children under 13 free.
    Student rate available.

√Limited Gift Shop
√Free Parking

Mackinac Maritime Park
Mackinaw City, Mich. 49701
Phone (616) 436-5563
Dr. Eugene Petersen, Director

48

MICHIGAN, SAULT STE. MARIE
Museum Ship Valley Camp

Steamship

Location: Six blocks east of the Soo Locks in Sault Ste. Marie.

Vessels: This typical Great Lakes freighter was built in 1917 by the American Shipbuilding Co. of Lorain, Ohio for the Hanna Mining Co. The 11,500 ton, coal-burning vessel is powered by a triple expansion steam engine that provided 1,800 horsepower. Until she was moved to her present berth, she was used to move bulk cargoes such as coal, iron ore and grain through the Great Lakes. A tour of the Valley Camp covers many parts of the ship from the forward pilot house to the engine room aft. In the No. 3 cargo hold is the Great Lakes Marine Hall of Fame. Here one can see a growing collection of artifacts relating to the maritime history of the Lakes.

Schedule: Daily, May 1 to October 15, 10:00 A. M. to 6:00 P. M. During July and August open from 9:00 A. M. to 8:00 P. M.

Admission: Adults $1.50, Children 50c, under 6 free.
Group rate available.

√Refreshments
√Gift Shop
√Free Parking

S.S. Valley Camp
P.O. Box 1668
Sault Ste. Marie, Mich. 49783
Phone (906) 632-3658
Thomas Manse, Director

√Memberships available on request.

49

Location: In Levee Park at the foot of Main Street in Winona, on the banks of the Mississippi River.

Vessels: Sponsored by the Winona County Historical Society, the woodhulled, sternwheel steamboat Julius C. Wilkie houses a museum of river transportation history. There are scale models of famous river craft, the work of retired rivermen. The collection of Robert Fulton material is particularly complete. Examples of steam engines, bells, wheels and other boat machinery are on exhibit. The Society has several other historic sites in the area including the 1850 Willard Bunnell House at Homer, Minn.

Schedule: May through October, Daily, 9:00 A. M. to 5:00 P. M. Sundays, 10:00 A. M. to 6:00 P. M.

Admission: Adults $1.25, Students 75c, (Children (under 12) 25c. No charge for Top Deck Galley dining area. Group rates available (by appointment).

Special Events: Steamboat Days celebration in July. Features parades, powerboat races and stage shows.

√Refreshments Julius C. Wilkie Steamboat Museum
√Restaurant c/o Dr. L. I. Younger
√Free Parking Winona, Minn. 55987
√Picnic Area Phone (507) 452-4570 Reservations: 454-2723

NEW JERSEY, HACKENSACK
Submarine Memorial Assoc. (U.S.S. Ling)

Submarine

John A. Sees

Location: The Ling is berthed on the Hackensack River near the intersection of Court and River Streets.

Vessels: Commissioned on June 8, 1945, the Ling (SS 297) made one patrol of the Atlantic during World War II. From 1946 to 1960 she was in reserve at New London. In 1962, the Ling was assigned to the Brooklyn Navy Yard for training Naval Reserve submariners. Stricken from the Navy Register in 1971, she was donated to the Submarine Memorial Assoc. and arrived at Hackensack in 1973. Tours through the 312 ft. vessel are conducted by submarine combat veterans of World War II. At the site is a memorial to all lost submariners, and a growing collection of pictures and materials from World War II sub operations.

Schedule: Daily, year round, 10:00 A. M. to 6:00 P. M.

Admission: Adults $1.50, Children 75c, under 5 free.
Group rate available.

Special Events: Services on Memorial Day, July 4th, Veterans Day

√Refreshments
√Gift Shop
√Free Parking

The Submarine Memorial Assoc.
P.O. Box 395
Hackensack, N. J. 07602
Phone (201) 488-9770
Harry G. Gooding, Jr., Director, President

Bill Lingard

Location: On Riverside Drive in Clayton on the St. Lawrence River in the heart of the Thousand Islands region.

Exhibits: The Thousand Islands Museum is housed in the old Town Hall of Clayton. The extensive displays include a reconstruction of Clayton of the 1890's with old stores, houses, school, hotel; equipped from the Museum's collection of antiquities. There is also a large collection of St. Lawrence River memorabilia with pictures, prints, documents, marine items, duck decoys, and the Muskie Hall of Fame. A visit to the Thousand Islands Museum can be combined with one to the nearby Thousand Islands Shipyard Museum.

Schedule: June through October, Daily, 10:00 A. M. to 9:00 P. M.

Admission: Adults 75c, Children 25c, under 6 free.
Group rate available.

Special Events: Thousand Islands Antique Boat Show and Antique Outboard Demonstration, August 7-8, 1976.

√Gift Shop
√City Parking
√Picnic Area

Thousand Islands Museum
Riverside Drive
Clayton, N. Y. 13624
Phone (315) 686-5794

√Memberships available on request.

52

Photo by Joseph Young, Jr.

Location: On Mary Street in Clayton near the Municipal Dock on the St. Lawrence River.

Exhibits: The new Thousand Islands Shipyard Museum is considered the only fresh water museum of its kind with emphasis on antique power craft. Within the main building is an exhibit of small vessels ranging from canoes to larger power boats. There is a unique collection of antique outboard motors as well as many items of nautical hardware. The Museum is currently expanding into the lumber yard adjacent to its present site. In the photograph the present building is at the right with the new area encompassing the peninsula to the left. Additional historical displays can be seen at the nearby Thousand Islands Museum located in the Old Town Hall on Riverside Drive.

Schedule: Daily, June to September, 10:00 A. M. to 5:00 P. M.

Admission: Adults 75c, Children 25c, under 6 free.
Group rate available.

Special Events: Thousand Islands Antique Boat Show and Antique Outboard Demonstration August 7-8, 1976.

√Gift Shop
√Free Parking
√Picnic Area

Thousand Islands Shipyard Museum
Mary Street
Clayton, N. Y. 13624
Phone (315) 686-4104
Bolling W. Haxall, Chairman

√Memberships available on request.

Community Photo Studio

Location: On Main Street (Route 25A) in Cold Spring Harbor, on the
North Shore of Long Island, two miles west of Huntington.

Exhibits: During the years 1836 to 1862, Cold Spring Harbor was
home port to a small whaling fleet. The Whaling Museum Society was organized in 1936 to preserve the maritime heritage
of that time. A fully equipped whale boat is displayed just inside
the building entrance. The 19th Century whaling era is recalled
with exhibits of whaling apparatus and numerous prints, pictures
and maps. The Walter K. Earle Room contains a fine collection
of scrimshaw with over 400 pieces on display. Here also is
housed a growing library of books and pamphlets related to
whaling. Other exhibits of interest include a fine collection of
sailors knots, navigation instruments and ships tools, and a
diorama of the town as it appeared during the whaling period.

Schedule: Weekends, year round, 11:00 A. M. to 5:00 P. M.
Weekdays, late-June-Labor Day, 11:00 A. M. to 5:00 P. M.
Tours by advance appointment, year round.

Admission: Adults 50c, Children (6-14) 25c, under 6 free.

√Gift Shop   Whaling Museum Society
√Free Parking   Cold Spring Harbor, N. Y. 11724
                                    Phone (516) 367-3418
                                    Gerard W. Dempsey, Jr., Exec. Director

Durling Studio

Location: Boat departs from the Steel Pier in Lake George Village, not far from Exit 21 of the Northway.

Vessels: The Minne-Ha-Ha is named after the first true steamboat to sail on Lake George. The 200-ton vessel was built by the Lake George Steamboat Co. in 1969 and made her maiden voyage on August 2 of that year. The entire engineroom is in a sunken area 3 feet below the main deck and is surrounded by glass through which passengers can see the machinery in operation.

Schedule: Daily, June 19 through Labor Day. The boat makes six cruises, about 1 hour in length starting at 10:00 A. M. Moonlight Cruise: June 26 through Labor Day, Sunday through Wednesday. Two hour trip with Dixieland band leaves at 9:00 P. M. Longer tours of Lake George can be made on the diesel boats Ticonderoga and Mohican.

Fare: Adults $2.75, Children $1.25, under 5 free.
Moonlight Cruise: Adults $6.00, Children $3.00, under 5 free. Group rate available.

√Refreshments on ships
√Gift Shop on ships
√Free Parking

Lake George Steamboat Co., Inc.
P.O. Box 551
Lake George, N. Y. 12845
Phone (518) 668-5777
William P. Dow, Manager

Hope Wright

Location: The museum, model shop, art gallery, book store and other shops are located on or close to Fulton Street near the East River. Ships are berthed nearby at Piers 15 and 16.

Vessels: Eight ships are in the Seaport display, representing both sail and steam. Of special note are the two square-rigged sailing vessels Peking and Wavertree, now undergoing restoration. Steam powered vessels are represented by the ferry Gen. William Hart, the steam lighter Aqua and the tug Mathilda. The Ambrose lightship houses an exhibit on modern port activities.

Exhibits: The aim of the Seaport Museum is to restore an area of several blocks of early 19th century waterfront in lower Manhattan. The museum at 16 Fulton Street features displays of New York's maritime history, such as photos, paintings, and ship models.

Schedule: Daily, year round, except Christmas, Thanksgiving and New Year's Day. Noon to 6:00 P. M. Pier 16 summer hours, 9:00 A. M. to 9:00 P. M.

Admission: Free, except for Wavertree for which the charge is Adults $1.00, Children 50c, under 5 free, and Peking — Adults $1.50, Children 75c, under 7 free.

Special Events: The Museum maintains an extensive program of free events including art and antique shows, concerts and visiting ships.

√Refreshments
√Restaurant
√Gift Shop
√City Parking
√Picnic Area on Pier 16

South Street Seaport Museum
16 Fulton Street
New York, N. Y. 10038
Phone (212) 766-9020

√Memberships available on request.

New York State Dept. of Commerce

Location: On Main Street in the historic town of Sag Harbor, about 100 miles east of New York City.

Exhibits: Established in 1936, the Whaling Museum is housed in the former Masonic Temple, built in 1845. One enters the building through the jawbones of a whale. There are many displays relating to Sag Harbor's days as an important whaling port. Here one can see a fine collection of harpoons and whaling tools. Log books, paintings and scrimshaw are exhibited. Other rooms in the Museum contain many interesting furnishings. Outside is a whaleboat and three large kettles used to produce whale oil (try-works).

Schedule: Daily, May 15 to Sept. 30. Weekdays, 10:00 A. M. to 5:00 P. M. Sundays, 2:00 P. M. to 5:00 P. M.

Admission: Adults $1.00, Children 50c, under 6 free. Group rate available.

√Refreshments
√Gift Shop

Suffolk County Whaling Museum
P.O. Box 327A
Sag Harbor, N. Y. 11963
Phone (516) 725-0770
Walter B. Stearns, Curator

√Memberships available on request.

57

G & M Photos

Location: The Museum is housed in the former Canal Terminal building just off Route 4 in Whitehall (formerly Skenesborough).

Vessels: At the rear of the main building is the hull of the U.S.S. Ticonderoga, built in 1812. The vessel was in the battle of Plattsburgh in September 1814. The hull was raised from Lake Champlain in 1958.

Exhibits: The Museum contains many exhibits relating to Whitehall's title as the birthplace of the U.S. Navy. Of note is a scale model portraying Skenesborough Harbor in 1776 where twelve of the first naval craft were built. There are a number of models of lake boats and a diorama of the early canal locks at this site. Here one can see artifacts dating from the heyday of lake transportation. The Admiral Potter Room features items on his famous trip around the world.

Schedule: Daily, June 15 to Labor Day, 10:00 A. M. to 5:00 P. M. Rest of year by appointment.

Admission: Adults 75c, Children 25c.
Group rate available.

√Gift Shop
√Picnic Area
√Picnic Area

Skenesborough Museum
Whitehall, N. Y. 12887
Phone (518) 499-0458 or 499-0754
Doris B. Morton, Director

NORTH CAROLINA, CAROLINA BEACH
Blockade Runner Museum

Nautical Museum

Photo by Frank Trexler

Location: On U.S. 421 just north of Carolina Beach, and about 15 miles south of Wilmington.

Exhibits: The Blockade Runner Museum tells the story of the over 2,000 ships that attempted to reach the Carolina ports through the Northern blockade during the Civil War. There are detailed dioramas with audio and light explaining the blockade running operations. A 40-foot diorama of Fort Fisher shows the role of this strategic fortification to blockade running and the protection of Wilmington. There are exhibits of artifacts obtained by divers from sunken wrecks of blockade runners. Fourteen ship models show the fast ships which were 20 years ahead of their time. The Museum brings to life an interesting aspect of the Civil War.

Schedule: Daily, year round, 9:00 A. M. to 5:00 P. M.
Closed Christmas Day.
Open other times by appointment for groups of 25 or more.

Admission: Adults $1.50, Children 75c, under 6 free.
Group rate available.

√Gift Shop
√Free Parking
√Picnic Area

Blockade Runner Museum
P.O. Drawer Q
Carolina Beach, N.C. 28428
Phone (919) 458-5746
John H. Foard, Director

Location: The ship is moored on the west bank of the Cape Fear River in Wilmington, across from the downtown area.

Vessels: The U.S.S. North Carolina (BB-55) was completed in 1941 at the Brooklyn Navy Yard. She served throughout the Pacific during World War II and in 1961 was brought to Wilmington as a war memorial. Estimated time to tour the ship is 75 minutes. Two of three 16-in. gun turrets can be visited as well as one engine room, small gun mounts, living areas, and conning tower. A new exhibit is a restored Kingfisher float plane. "The Immortal Showboat," an exciting outdoor drama with sound and light effects, is presented nightly during summer.

Schedule: Daily, year round. Labor Day-May, 8:00 A. M. to approx. sunset. June-Labor Day, 8:00 A. M. to 8:00 P. M. Outdoor drama nightly at 9:00 P. M., June-Labor Day.

Admission: Adults $1.25, Children (6-11) 50c, under 6 free. Admission to outdoor drama. Adults $1.50, Children (6-11) 75c, under 6 free.

Special Events: Annual Memorial Day service on board ship.

√Refreshments   U.S.S. North Carolina Battleship Memorial
√Gift Shop   P.O. Box 417
√Free Parking   Wilmington, N. C. 28401
√Picnic Area   Phone (919) 762-1829
                   Capt. C. B. Jennings, U.S.N. (ret.), Director

OHIO, CINCINNATI
Delta Queen

Operating Steamboat

Bill Muster

Location: The Delta Queen cruises mainly on the Ohio and Mississippi Rivers, with some trips on the Tennessee River. Principal starting points are Cincinnati, St. Louis and New Orleans.

Vessels: Built in 1926 for service on the Sacramento River from San Francisco to Sacramento, the Delta Queen is America's only overnight paddlewheel steamboat. Legislation passed by Congress allows operation until November 1, 1978. Current plans call for a renewed effort to get a permanent exemption from the 1966 Safety at Sea Law. A new steamboat, the twenty million dollar Mississippi Queen, will join the Delta Queen in 1976.

Schedule: In 1976, there will be a full schedule of cruises starting with short trips out of New Orleans from Feb. 1-April 16, and ending with more New Orleans cruises, Nov. 7-Jan. 2, 1977. Write for complete schedule.

Fare: Depends on trip and type of accommodation.

Special Events: Annual Steamboat Race every May in Louisville between the Delta Queen and the Belle of Louisville. Historic events and civic celebrations often occur at landing places during trips.

√Meals on boat
√Gift Shop on boat
√Overnight Accommodations on boat

Green Line Steamers, Inc.
322 E. Fourth Street
Cincinnati, Ohio 45202
Phone (513) 621-1445

Ohio Historical Society

Location: On Front Street near the Muskingum River in Marietta. One block away is the Campus Martius Museum, which depicts the story of the first settlement in the Northwest Territory.

Vessels: Built in 1918 at Pittsburgh, Pa., the W. P. Snyder was used primarily to push coal barges on the Monongahela River. The 175-ft. long vessel was presented to the Ohio Historical Society in 1955. Moored alongside the Ohio River Museum, the boat is open to visitors. A replica of a flat boat of the 1800's is moored near the W. P. Snyder.

Exhibits: The Ohio River Museum is a unique structure composed of three separate exhibit buildings elevated on stilts to provide flood protection from the Muskingum River. The displays include information on the river's natural history, the "golden age of the steamboat" and the impact of the river on man and man on the river. A compact multi-media theater presents a program entitled "The River". The Ohio River Museum is operated by the Ohio Historical Society.

Schedule: Daily, year round, Monday through Saturday, 9:00 A. M. to 5:00 P. M., Sundays, 1:00 P. M. to 5:00 P. M.

Admission: Adults $1.00, Children 50c, Children 12 and under accompanied by an adult are admitted free.

Special Events: Annual meeting of Sons and Daughters of Pioneer Rivermen held in September.

√Gift Shop
√Free Parking

Ohio River Museum
Front Street
Marietta, Ohio 45750
Phone (614) 373-3717
Mrs. Catherine Remley, Curator

Bradley Gelinas

Location: At 480 Main Street, U.S. 6, on the shore of Lake Erie. Vermilion is about 40 miles west of Cleveland.

Exhibits: The Great Lakes Historical Society was founded in 1944 to preserve the history and folklore of the Lakes region. The Society's museum exhibits a fine collection of ship models, marine relics, paintings and photographs. On display is a complete bridge and engine room console from a Great Lakes iron ore carrier and a 500 h.p. steam engine from a tug boat. The Perry room contains artifacts from the War of 1812. In Vermilion, the Harbour Town 1837 historic area, contains many homes of early lake captains and other buildings related to the nautical past of Lake Erie.

Schedule: Daily, March-Dec., 11:00 A. M. to 5:00 P. M. Weekends only, Jan.-Feb.

Admission: Adults $1.00, Children 50c, under 6 free. Group rate available.

Special Events: Festival Model Boat Show and Contest in June.

√Gift Shop   Great Lakes Historical Society
√Free Parking   480 Main Street
                              Vermilion, Ohio 44089
                              Phone (216) 967-3467
                              Arthur N. O'Hara, Business Manager
          √Memberships available on request.

63

Columbia River Maritime Museum

Location: At 16th & Exchange Streets in Astoria. The old lightship Columbia is moored at the foot of 17th Street just below the Museum.

Vessels: Lightship #88, the Columbia, was completed in 1908 at Camden, N. J. From 1909 to 1961 she was on station off the mouth of the Columbia River and other locations on the Northwest coast.

Exhibits: Opened in 1963, the Museum is located in the former Astoria City Hall. A visit brings to mind the exciting days of the stern and side wheelers on the Columbia. There is a fine collection of models, paintings, navigation instruments and whaling artifacts. A featured exhibit is the revolving beacon of the old North Head lighthouse.

Schedule: Daily, May-October, 10:30 A. M. to 5:00 P. M.
Closed Mondays November to May.

Admission: Museum: Adults 50c, Children 25c.
Lightship: Adults 35c, Children 20c.

Special Events: Lectures and maritime history programs.

√Free Parking

Columbia River Maritime Museum
16th & Exchange Streets
Astoria, Ore. 97103
Phone (503) 325-2323
Rolf Klep, Director

√Memberships available on request.

NAUTICAL MUSEUM DIRECTORY
GUEST COUPONS
Discounts shown on reverse side

GUEST COUPON
BOSTON TEA PARTY SHIP & MUSEUM
Boston, Mass.

GUEST COUPON
GREAT LAKES HISTORICAL SOCIETY
Vermilion, Ohio

GUEST COUPON
REVOLUTIONARY WAR FRIGATE ROSE
Newport, R. I.

GUEST COUPON
SHELBURNE MUSEUM
Shelburne, Vt.

GUEST COUPON
SUBMARINE MEMORIAL ASSOC.
Hackensack, N. J.

GUEST COUPON
U.S.S. ALABAMA BATTLESHIP COMMISSION
Mobile, Ala.

GUEST COUPON
U.S.S. MASSACHUSETTS
Fall River, Mass.

NAUTICAL MUSEUM DIRECTORY
GUEST COUPONS

BOSTON TEA PARTY SHIP & MUSEUM
Boston, Mass.
Regular Adm.: Adult $1.50, Child 75c
With this coupon: 20% discount on adult or child admission
Valid from May 1976 to Oct. 1976
rates subject to change

GREAT LAKES HISTORICAL SOCIETY
Vermilion, Ohio
Regular Adm.: Adult $1.00, Child 50c
With this coupon: 1/3 reduction on adult or child admission
Valid from June 1976 to Dec. 1976
rates subject to change

REVOLUTIONARY WAR FRIGATE ROSE
Newport, R. I.
Regular Adm.: Adult $1.00, Child 75c
With this coupon: 10% discount on adult or child admission
Valid from May 1976 to Dec. 1976
rates subject to change

SHELBURNE MUSEUM
Shelburne, Vt.
Regular Adm.: Adult $4.00, Child $2.00
With thi scoupon: Adult $3.50, Child $1.75
Valid from May 15, 1976 ot Oct. 15, 1976
rates subject to change

SUBMARINE MEMORIAL ASSOC.
Hackensack, N. J.
Regular Adm.: Adult $1.50, Child 75c
With this coupon: 25% discount on adult or child admission
Valid from May 1976 to Dec. 1977
rates subject to change

U.S.S. ALABAMA BATTLESHIP COMMISSION
Mobile, Ala.
Regular Adm.: Adult $2.00, Child 50c
With this coupon: A discount on adult or child admission
Valid from June 1976 to June 1977
rates subject to change

U.S.S. MASSACHUSETTS
Fall River, Mass.
Regular Adm.: Adult $3.00, Child $1.25
With this coupon: 50% discount on adult, 40 on child admission
Valid from June 1, 1976 to Dec. 31, 1976
rates subject to change

Pennsylvania Historical & Museum Commission

Location: Permanently berthed at the foot of State Street, overlooking the Lake, in Erie.

Vessels: The U.S.S. Niagara was one of six small war vessels built on the shores of Lake Erie to provide a naval force against British squadrons operating on the Great Lakes during the War of 1812. In the Battle of Lake Erie, the ship was Commander Perry's second flagship. The Niagara is a square-rigged warship of 34 guns. The reconstruction dates from 1913 and is now a state property administered by the Pennsylvania Historical & Museum Commission in Harrisburg. Adjacent to the Niagara is the prow section of the U.S.S. Wolverine, first iron warship of the U.S. Navy on the Great Lakes.

Schedule: Daily, except Mondays, 8:30 A. M. to 5:00 P. M. Sundays, 1:00 P. M. to 5:00 P. M. Winter hours, 9:00 A. M. to 4:30 P. M. weekdays and 1:00 P. M. to 4:30 P. M. Sundays. Closed certain Holidays.

Admission: Free.

√Free Parking

U.S.S. Niagara
Foot of State Street
Erie, Pa. 16500
Phone (814) 454-2300
William Dudenhoefer, Director

65

Philadelphia Maritime Museum

Location: At 321 Chestnut Street, just off Independence Square in Philadelphia.

Exhibits: Founded in 1960, the Philadelphia Maritime Museum traces nautical history from the time of early sailing ships to modern vessels. There is emphasis on the maritime heritage of the Delaware River Valley. At the Museum is an outstanding display of ship models, prints, paintings and nautical artifacts. The "Underwater Man" exhibit traces man's attempts to live, work, play and explore under the sea. At Penn's Landing on the Delaware River, a few blocks away, is berthed the Gazela Primeiro, a sailing ship preserved by the Museum.

Schedule: Daily, year round, Monday-Saturday, 10:00 A. M. to 5:00 P. M. Sunday, 1:00 P. M. to 5:00 P. M. Closed Christmas, New Year's Day and Easter.

Admission: Adults $1.00, Children under 12, 50c.
Group rate available.

√Gift Shop
√City Parking

Philadelphia Maritime Museum
321 Chestnut Street
Philadelphia, Pa. 19106
Phone (215) WA-5-5439
Richard K. Page, Director

PENNSYLVANIA, PHILADELPHIA   **Sailing Ship**
Gazela Primeiro

Philadelphia Maritime Museum

Location: In August, 1976, the ship will arrive at its new berth in Penn's Landing, off Delaware Ave. in downtown Philadelphia.

Vessels: Built in 1883, the Gazela Primeiro is a 324-ton barkentine. She served for nearly 90 years in the Portuguese fishing fleet on the North Atlantic cod-fish grounds. On board the ship one can visit the cramped quarters of the fisherman and the galley where the ship's cook prepared the monotonous diet of cod in numerous ways. On deck are the small dories used by the fisherman to gather their catch. The Gazela Primeiro is preserved in sailing condition by the Philadelphia Maritime Museum, 321 Chestnut Street, several blocks from where the ship is berthed.

Schedule: Daily, Memorial Day through Labor Day, Noon to 5:00 P. M. (Open August 1976 at Penn's Landing).

Admission: Adults $1.00, Children 50c.

Special Event. Participation in Operation Sail, July 1976.

√Gift Shop
√City Parking

Philadelphia Maritime Museum
321 Chestnut Street
Philadelphia, Pa. 19106
Phone: Museum: WA-5-5439
Richard K. Page, Director

U.S.S. Olympia
U.S.S. Becuna

Philadelphia Convention & Tourist Bureau

Location: The ships are berthed at Penn's Landing on the Delaware River in Philadelphia.

Vessels: The U.S.S. Olympia is the last survivor of the "New Navy" of the 1880's and 1890's. She was launched in 1891 at San Francisco and commissioned in 1895. During the Spanish-American War, the Olympia was Commodore Dewey's flagship at the Battle of Manila Bay. In 1922 she was decommissioned after service during World War I. The Cruiser Olympia Association has restored the ship as a museum. Several areas of the ship can be visited including Admiral Dewey's quarters. On exhibit are naval uniforms, medals, flags, ship models and relics of naval history. U.S.S. Becuna is a submarine used in World War II.

Schedule: Mid-April to Thanksgiving, Monday through Saturday, 10:00 A. M. to 4:00 P. M. Sundays, 11:00 A. M. to 6:00 P. M.

Admission: BOTH SHIPS: Adults $2.50, Children (under 12) $1.25.

√Refreshments nearby	U.S.S. Olympia
√Restaurants nearby	Penn's Landing
√Gift Shop	Philadelphia, Pa. 19106
√City Parking	Phone (215) WA 2-1898
	Casper J. Knight, Jr., Director

RHODE ISLAND, NEWPORT
Revolutionary War Frigate Rose

Reconstructed Vessel

Location: The ship is berthed in the Inner Harbor at America's Cup Ave., in the historic city of Newport.

Vessels: H.M.S. Rose is a full-sized reconstruction of the British 24-gun frigate that blockaded ports along the East Coast during 1774-1779. By her close blockade of Rhode Island, she brought about an Act of Congress that set up the Continental Navy in October 1775. Displacement is 500 tons and the length of the hull is 125 ft. Below deck one can see the authentically furnished Great Cabin, a collection of ship models and Colonial military exhibits. The Rose is the only example of a Revolutionary War ship afloat today, but she will soon be joined by a replica of the 12-gun Continental sloop Providence, the first command of John Paul Jones.

Schedule: Daily, May-October, 10:00 A. M. to Sunset.
Weekends rest of year.

Admission: Adults $1.00, Children 75c, under 5 free.

Special Events: Annual celebration of Continental Navy's birthday, 13th October. Sea Chanty concerts, July and August, Fridays at 7:30 P. M. Providence will tour Colonial seaports in 1976.

√Picnic Area
√Gift Shop
√Free Parking

Seaport '76
60 Church Street
Newport, R. I. 02840
Phone (401) 846-1776
John F. Millar, Curator

Keller Studio

Location: At 340 East Main Street in Fredricksburg, about 60 miles north of San Antonio and about 70 miles west of Austin. Fredericksburg is an old German settlement with many historic structures.

Exhibits: The Admiral Nimitz Center, a State of Texas museum, is located in the old Nimitz Hotel, built by the grandfather of the late Fleet Admiral. Started by local citizens, the museum contains a growing number of exhibits honoring Chester Nimitz and all the fighting forces of the war in the Pacific. Of interest is a "Please Touch" room where visitors are invited to handle and examine the relics. There are a number of exhibits from retired naval vessels including a combat information center from the destroyer Frankford, a mast from the destroyer Foote and the conning tower from the sub Pintado. Exhibits and displays tell the story of the naval career of Admiral Nimitz. Other items of note are a Japanese Val dive bomber and an Alligator landing craft. A multi-screen audio presentation tells about the museum and the career of Admiral Nimitz.

Schedule: Daily, year round, 8:00 A. M. to 5:00 P. M. Closed Thanksgiving, Christmas and New Year's Day.

Admission: Free.

√Gift Shop
√Free Parking

Admiral Nimitz Center
P. O. Box 777
Fredericksburg, Texas 78624
Phone (512) 997-4379
Douglass H. Hubbard, Director

Location: The ships are berthed at Seawolf Park on Pelican Island, a short drive from downtown Galveston via the Pelican Island Bridge.

Vessels: U.S.S. Cavalla (SS-244) was commissioned in 1944 and made six patrols before the end of World War II. Her torpedoes sank the large Japanese carrier Shokaku, for which Cavalla received the Presidential Unit Citation. In later years she was outfitted as a killer submarine to detect and destroy enemy underwater craft. U.S.S. Stewart was built in 1944 by Brown Shipbuilding of Houston, Texas. The destroyer escort (DE-238) saw duty in the North Atlantic. In 1974 she joined the Cavalla at Seawolf Park. Besides exhibits on submarine warfare, one can see a Navy F-1 jet fighter and an M-41 tank. The ships are operated by the Submarine Seawolf Commission.

Schedule: Daily, year round, 10:00 A. M. until dusk.

Admission: Seawolf Park: $1.00 per car.
    Ships: Adults $1.00, Children (under 12) 50c.

√Refreshments   Submarine Seawolf Commission
√Gift Shop on Stewart   P.O. Box 1575
√Parking $1.00   Galveston, Texas 77550
√Picnic Area

TEXAS, HOUSTON
Battleship Texas

Warship

Harper-Leiper Studios

Location: The Texas is moored at the San Jacinto Battle Grounds, southeast of Houston via the Gulf Freeway and State Routes 225 and 134.

Vessels: Texas was the first State to preserve its namesake battleship. The Texas rests in a special slip off the Houston Ship Channel. Completed in 1914 at Newport News, Va., she was the last major fighting ship to use reciprocating engines. After extensive service during World Wars I and II, the Texas was placed in its permanent berth in 1948. The Admiral Nimitz Room, the Trophy Room and the Cruiser Houston Room on the ship contain exhibits of note. A Talk Hour of 12, 3-minute tapes tells the story of the ship. Other displays honor the Texan Navy, which was active when Texas was fighting for its independence from Mexico.

Schedule: Daily, year round, May 1 through Labor Day, 10:00 A. M. to 7:00 P. M. Labor Day through April 30, 11:00 A. M. to 5:00 P. M.

Admission: Adults $1.00, Children (6-11) 50c, under 6 free.

√Refreshments
√Gift Shop
√Free Parking
√Picnic Area

The Battleship Texas Commission
San Jacinto Battlegrounds
Houston, Texas
C. H. Taylor, Chairman

72

Shelburne Museum

Location: The Museum is on Route 7 in Shelburne, a few miles south of Burlington.

Vessels: The S.S. Ticonderoga was built at Shelburne Harbor in 1906 for the Champlain Transportation Co. She was in service on Lake Champlain until 1953. In that year the 220 ft., 892-ton vessel was moved four miles inland to its present site.

Exhibits: Besides the nautical items on display in the Ticonderoga, there is a fine collection of paintings, prints and other marine exhibits in the old Colchester Reef Lighthouse. This building was transported from its location in the middle of Lake Champlain to its present site adjacent to the Ticonderoga in 1952. Some of the many fine buildings on the museum grounds display marine woodcarvings and various other nautical memorabilia.

Schedule: Daily, May 15 through October 15, 9:00 A. M. to 5:00 P. M.

Admission: Museum Admission: Adults $4.00, Children $2.00, under 6 free.
Group rate available.

√Refreshments
√Restaurant
√Gift Shop
√Free Parking
√Picnic Area

Shelburne Museum, Inc.
Shelburne, Vt. 05482
Phone (802) 985-3344
Kenneth E. Wheeling, Director

Jamestown Festival Park

Location: Adjacent to Jamestown National Historic Site, a short distance from Williamsburg via the Colonial Parkway.

Vessels: On December 20, 1606, three square-rigged merchant ships, the Susan Constant, the Godspeed and the Discovery, sailed from Blackwall, England. Arrival at Jamestown was on May 13, 1607. The anchorage of the replicas is about 1 mile upstream from the original landing site. The present ships were built during 1956-1957 for the Jamestown Festival Park. The Susan Constant is 111 ft. in overall length with a displacement of 100 tons. The two other vessels are considerably smaller. A costumed interpreter is aboard to explain the ships and answer questions.

Schedule: Daily, year round, except Christmas and New Year's Day, 9:00 A. M. to 5:00 P. M.

Admission: Admission to Jamestown Festival Park:
Adults $2.00, Children (7-12) 75c, under 7 free.

√Refreshments
√Restaurant
√Gift Shop
√Free Parking
√Picnic Area

Jamestown Festival Park
P.O. Drawer JF
Williamsburg, Va. 23185
Phone (804) 229-1607
Parke Rouse, Jr., Exec. Director

The Mariners Museum

Location: The Museum entrance is at the intersection of Route 60 and J. Clyde Morris Blvd. (Route 312) in Newport News, minutes from Exit 9B or Exit 9A on Interstate 64.

Exhibits: Founded in 1930 by Archer M. Huntington, The Mariners Museum features the most extensive nautical collection in the country. The main building is situated on an 550-acre site with a large lake. International in scope, the exhibits cover many areas of the history of man's conquest of the sea. Over 1,000 models show the development of water transportation. The figurehead display features 85 fine examples of this form of art. The pictorial collection contains thousands of items which provide for frequently changing exhibitions in the galleries. There are displays of ship decorations, navigation instruments and naval weapons. Over 200 objects can be seen in the new Decorative Arts Gallery. A new small craft collection is made up of coastal rescue craft, sailboats, canoes, a gondola and other small vessels.

Schedule: Daily, year round, Weekdays, 9:00 A. M. to 5:00 P. M. Sundays, Noon to 5:00 P. M. Closed Christmas Day.

Admission: Adults $1.50, Children (6-16) 75c, under 6 free.
Group rates (15 or more persons) Adults 75c, Children 50c.

√Gift Shop
√Free Parking
√Picnic Area

The Mariners Museum
Newport News, Va. 23606
Phone (703) 595-0368

Fariss Pictures

Location: 2 High Street, overlooking the Elizabeth River, in Portsmouth.

Exhibits: The Museum portrays the history of the nation's oldest naval shipyard, the Portsmouth area, and the armed services of the region. Ship models, uniforms, arms of all types, from early muskets to the Polaris missile and various naval memorabilia are on display. The history of the famous C.S.S. Virginia (originally the U.S.S. Merrimac), which fought its historic battle with the Monitor in nearby waters, is shown. Over 35 models of ships, many of which were built at the naval shipyard, are exhibited. Berthed near the Museum is the Lightship Portsmouth.

Schedule: Daily, except Mondays, year round. Tues.-Sat., 10:00 A. M. to 5:00 P. M. Sundays, 2:00 P. M. to 5:00 P. M. Closed December 25, and January 1.

Admission: Free.

√Gift Shop
√Metered Parking
  (free Sundays)

Portsmouth Naval Shipyard Museum
P.O. Box 248
Portsmouth, Va. 23705
Phone (703) 393-8591
Mrs. Alice C. Hanes, Administrator

WISCONSIN, MANITOWOC
Manitowoc Maritime Museum

Location: The Museum is at 809 South 8th Street in the city center. The submarine is berthed nearby in the Manitowoc River.

Vessels: Commissioned in 1944, the Cobia (SS 245) made 6 war patrols in the Pacific. In August 1970, the ship was dedicated at Manitowoc as a memorial to submariners. The 312-foot vessel is maintained in its original condition and is open for guided tours.

Exhibits: The Museum features displays on the maritime history of the Great Lakes. There are ship models, photographs, navigation instruments and other maritime artifacts. Of note is a lake steamer pilot house built from items taken from various ships. The submarine collection includes exhibits on the 28 undersea craft built at Manitowoc during World War II.

Schedule: Museum: Daily, June 1 to Sept. 7, 9:00 A. M. to 5:00 P. M. Rest of year, 11:00 A. M. to 4:00 P. M.
Submarine: Daily, June 1 to Sept. 7, 9:00 A. M. to 5:00 P. M. Rest of year, weekends. Weekdays by appointment for groups of 20 or more.

Admission: Museum: Adults $1.00, Children 50c, under 6 free. Combined Rate: Adults $2.50, Children $1.25.
Group rates available for 20 or more.

Special Events: International memorial services for submariners.

√Gift Shop
√Metered Parking at Museum
√Metered Parking at Sub.

Manitowoc Maritime Museum
809 South 8th Street
Manitowoc, Wisc. 54220
Phone (414) 684-8381

√Memberships available on request.

Maritime Museum

Location: At the North foot of Cypress Street in Vancouver.

Vessels: Located alongside the Maritime Museum in an impressive shelter structure, the Royal Canadian Mounted Police vessel St. Roch is a veteran of many years in the Arctic. Built in 1928, the ship was in use until the 1950's. She is the first ship to have navigated the Northwest Passage in both directions. A major restoration of the 104-foot wooden vessel has now been completed and the St. Roch is open for guided tours.

Exhibits: The Maritime Museum is a division of the Centennial Museum of Vancouver, located nearby. A series of colorful displays sets forth the many facets of the maritime history of Canada's west coast.

Schedule: Daily, year round, 10:00 A. M. to 5:30 P. M. Open all Holidays.

Admission: Adults 50c, Children 25c, under 5 free.

√Restaurant in
  Centennial Museum
√Gift Shop in
  Centennial Museum
√Free Parking
√Picnic Area Nearby

Maritime Museum
1905 Ogden Street
Vancouver, B.C., Canada Z6J 3J9
Phone (604) 736-9411

CANADA, HALIFAX, NOVA SCOTIA   **Nautical Museum**
Maritime Museum
Marine History Dept. of the Nova Scotia Museum

FIGUREHEAD OF H. M. S. "CONQUEROR"

R. E. Merrick, N. S. Museum

Location: The Maritime Museum is housed in the Cavalier Block within the Halifax Citadel overlooking Halifax Harbor.

Exhibits: Established in 1948, the Museum portrays the marine history of Nova Scotia in its various phases. There are exhibits on "The Golden Age of Sail" when local square-riggers traded throughout the globe and on trans-Atlantic and coastwise steam navigation. Other fields covered are the development of the fishing industry and the Navy in peace and war. A large marine library and photo collection are available to the serious researcher.

Schedule: Daily, year round, June 1 - September 1, 9:00 A. M. to 8:00 P. M. Rest of year, 10:00 A. M. to 5:00 P. M.

Admission: Free.

Special Events: Marine exhibit during summer at the Nova Scotia Museum, located within walking distance of the Citadel.

√Free Parking
√Refreshments

Nova Scotia Museum
Dept. of Marine History
1747 Summer Street
Halifax, Nova Scotia, Canada
Phone (902) 429-4610
Niels W. Jannasch, Curator

CANADA, SARNIA, ONTARIO
Pilot House Museum

Nautical Museum

Pilot House Museum

Location: On Highway 40, 5 miles south of Sarnia. Port Huron, Michigan is the nearest U.S. point to Sarnia.

Exhibits: The Pilot House Museum is contained within the bridge-house of the S.S. Imperial Hamilton, a Great Lakes tanker. Built in 1916, the Hamilton was in service until 1961. In 1963 the bridge structure was moved to its present site overlooking the St. Clair River. Inside the Museum one can view the restored officers' quarters, captain's cabin and wheel house. There is a large display of photographs of Great Lakes ships past and present. One can see models of sailing ships as well as more recent freighters and passenger steamers. Other exhibits include navigation instruments, life rings, logbooks and numerous items from Great Lakes vessels. New in 1975, is a 30-minute slide show on the nautical history of the area.

Schedule: June - September, Monday through Saturday, 9:00 A. M. to 5:00 P. M., Sundays, 2:00 P. M. to 5:00 P. M.

Admission: Adults 50c, Children 25c.
Group rate available.

√Free Parking
√Picnic Area

Pilot House Museum
2012 Wayne Street
Sarnia, Ontario, Canada
Phone (519) 344-6136
Malcolm McRae, Director

CANADA, TORONTO, ONTARIO
H.M.C.S. Haida

Warship

Ontario Ministry of Industry & Tourism

Location: H.M.C.S. Haida is berthed at Ontario Place, on Lake Ontario, next to the Canadian National Exhibition grounds, close to downtown Toronto.

Vessels: Ontario Place, a 96-acre cultural-leisure complex on 3 manmade islands, is the home of H.M.C.S. Haida, a Tribal Class Destroyer. The 3,000-ton vessel was built in Newcastle-on-Tyne, England and entered war service as a convoy escort to Murmansk. In 1944 she was in several actions off the coast of France. Haida served in the Korean War in 1953. Retired in 1963, the ship is now operated by the Ontario Place Corporation.

Schedule: H.M.C.S. Haida: May 22 to Sept. 6, Daily. Sept. 11 to Oct. 11, Weekends only. Open 10:30 A. M. to Sundown.

Admission: Ontario Place General Admission: Adults $1.50, Juniors (13-17) $1.00, Children with parent free.
H.M.C.S. Haida: Adults 50c, Children 25c.
Prices subject to change during the Canadian National Exhibition, latter part of August.

√Refreshments
√Restaurants
√Gift Shop at Ontario Place
√Parking $1.00
√Picnic Area

Ontario Place Corporation
8 York Street
Toronto, Ontario, Canada M5J 1R2
Phone (416) 965-6331

81

Marine Museum of Upper Canada

Location: At the east entrance of Exhibition Park overlooking Lake Ontario.

Vessels: The fully-restored 80-foot steam tug Ned Hanlan is situated in a dry berth beside the Museum. The 185-ton ship was built in 1932 and is open to visitors during the summer months.

Exhibits: Established in 1959, the Marine Museum tells the story of the shipping and waterways of the Great Lakes-St. Lawrence region of Central Canada. There are over 50 fine ship models and many exhibits of nautical artifacts. A noteworthy feature is the reconstruction of the navigation bridge of the famous steamer Cayuga.

Schedule: Daily, year round, Monday-Saturday, 9:30 A. M. to 5:00 P. M. Sundays and Holidays, Noon to 5:00 P. M.

Admission: Adults 50c, Children 25c, under 5 free.

Special Events: Periodic special exhibits.

√Restaurant,
  Luncheon weekdays
√Gift Shop
√Free Parking

Marine Museum of Upper Canada
Exhibition Park
Toronto 2B, Ontario, Canada
Phone (416) 531-4628
Alan Howard, Curator

INDEX OF LISTINGS

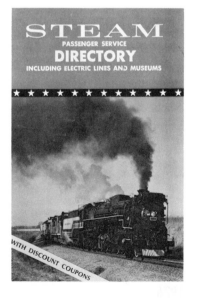

A D D E N D U M
(Data received too late for inclusion in main listings)

SOUTH CAROLINA, CHARLESTON **Warship**
U.S.S. Yorktown

The carrier Yorktown, known as "The Fighting Lady" of World War II, is now on display as the first unit of a developing Naval and Maritime Museum at Patriots Point on Charleston Harbor. Yorktown is open daily, year round, 9:00 A. M. to 6:00 P. M. Admission is charged.

For further information write:
> Patriots Point Development Auth.
> P.O. Box 634
> Charleston, S.C. 29402

Model by Charlie Notches, Oakland, N. J.

MERCHANT BRIG VOLANTE
NEW YORK 1853

A source for ship model kits, fittings, books, tools, plans and materials. Send 75c for our 64 page catalog.

*   *   *   *   *

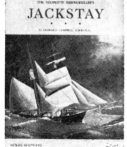

For beginners and the curious, there is **THE NEOPHYTE SHIPMODELLERS JACKSTAY, by George F. Campbell, M.R.I.N.A., 60 pages, 8½"x11", text and sketch by a foremost marine historian and artist. $3.45 postpaid.**

*   *   *   *   *

At the best hobby dealers, coast to coast.
Model Shipways Co., Inc., 39 West Fort Lee Rd., Bogota, N. J. 07603